MARCH OF THE COMPASSIONATE NEIGHBOR

MARCH OF THE COMPASSIONATE NEIGHBOR

Selected Poems

J. A. FAULKERSON

J. A. Faulkerson Books

CONTENTS

CHECKMATE   7

MARCH OF THE COMPASSIONATE NEIGHBOR   9

THE BANE OF THEIR DISDAIN   13

RETREAT OF THE CONQUERING OPPRESSOR   15

KAMALA, SPEAK!   17

NOW THAT YOU KNOW   21

MIC DROP   23

I AM   27

SOCIAL WORK   29

PEACEMAKERS WANTED, APPLY WITHIN   31

LEAN FORWARD, ENGAGE   33

UNCOMMITTED   37

TWO WORDS   39

CHARGE TO THE COMPASSIONATE COALITION   41

THE MAGNIFICENCE OF YOUR SINGLENESS 45

BALANCE 47

ABLE 49

CRITICAL RACE THEORY 51

TWO SIDES, TWO COINS 55

WAKANDA DREAMING 59

TRUE BUILD | A BLACK WALL STREET STORY 63

..... 77

MARCH OF THE COMPASSIONATE NEIGHBOR

Selected Poems

J. A. Faulkerson

MARCH OF THE COMPASSIONATE NEIGHBOR

Selected Poems

J. A. FAULKERSON

MARCH OF THE
COMPASSIONATE NEIGHBOR
Selected Poems

by
J. A. Faulkerson

ISBN: 979-8-9910333-2-9

First Printing

Published by
J. A. Faulkerson Books
Culturally Coded Content
www.jafaulkerson.com

The times that we live in
A call to make it right
Neighbor helping neighbor
Overcoming our collective plight
Don't allow the naysayers
To call Black History CRT
Unite with enlightened others
Demand racial amnesty

MARCH OF THE COMPASSIONATE NEIGHBOR

Selected Poems

J. A. FAULKERSON

Checkmate

The times that we live in
Require moments of reflection
Temporary pause to consider
Historical inflections
We weren't born
To be enslaved by the naysayer, the other
We all were made in His image
To be sister, brother

The times that we live in
Cause us to doubt our place
Wanting to be citizens of this country
Not members of a specific race
Don't get me wrong
Beautiful is the color black
But when they confine us to a color
They're suggesting we lack

The times that we live in
No reason to spat
Kindness, civility
A tip of the hat
Compassion and love

Should be the basis of our interactions
Making additions to the family
Not senseless subtractions

The times that we live in
A call to make it right
Neighbor helping neighbor
Overcoming our collective plight
Don't allow the naysayers
To call Black History CRT
Unite with enlightened others
Demand racial amnesty

The times that we live in
A perpetual game of chess they play
Enough of this nonsense
It's not the bed I wish to lay
By working together,
More can be great
Proclaim to the naysayers,
"Checkmate!"

March of the Compassionate Neighbor

Compassionate.

Neighborly.

Two words with different meanings but working toward the same result.

The Literati say they are adjectives that modify nouns. I say they become active verbs when they are embodied in a person, in a people.

There have been protests, there have been marches. The one I think about most is the 1963 *March on Washington*, where the keynote speaker was the Rev. Dr. Martin Luther, King, Jr.

This march produced results, specifically passage of the Civil Rights Act of 1964.

But then there was the one in 1965, at Selma's Edmund Pettis Bridge, where then Southern Nonviolent Coordinating Committee Chairman John Lewis and other black residents were beaten with sticks wielded by white police officers.

Bloody Sunday, they call it.

Black bodies bloodied by white lawmen, white lawmakers, for wanting to participate in the franchise – local, state and federal elections.

These are the marches I think about, the ones that resonate with me the most.

No, I wasn't there. I arrived in 1968, 16 days before an assassin's bullet ended Dr. King's life.

Nor was I there in October 1995, when Louis Farrakan invited Black American men and their non-black allies to something called the *Million Man March*.

I may have not been present that day, a small speck among the sea of black men, but my spirit was. Watching this event play out on TV, I prayed that the nation would look past Farrakan's fiery rhetoric to hear his admonishment to black men.

Black men, you must do more to stand in the gap for your black women, your black children, your American nation.

These marches had goals, righteous ones.

But then January 6, 2021, happened.

The *Stop the Steal* Rally.

An event organized by supporters of a former United States president.

The individuals who came to Washington that day weren't compassionate or neighborly.

If anything, these insurrectionists were livid, driven by hatred for their fellow man, their fellow compatriots, all because their candidate had lost his bid to serve a second term as the United States president.

The question that we, members of the US electorate, must ask ourselves is what hope did these insurrectionists have in reclaiming something that had not been stolen?

Why didn't they just stay home, accept the loss like so many others have done, support the peaceful transfer of presidential power?

That's what the citizens of democracies are expected to do when voters duly elect a new leader to office.

But that begs another question.

How are we supposed to act in times such as these?

Times when absolute truths, facts really, are ignored, disregarded.

Times when news of candidates' criminality, indiscretions, don't disqualify them from running for political office but instead allow them to lead by double digits in their party's statewide primary elections.

Times when marches led by the descendants of enslaved Africans are wrongly contrasted with one that served the purpose of one person, the defeated former president.

The Christian Bible admonishes us to do unto others as we would have others do unto us.

These united states of America can be great, but they can never be great again. That's because they have never been great.

Enshrined in the U.S. Constitution is a pledge to create a more perfect union.

Why?

Because our Native Americans ancestors had their land stolen from them.

Because our Black Americans ancestors were enslaved and oppressed.

Because our Asian American ancestors were relegated to concentration camps on US soil during World War II.

Nothing great about denying people's rights to life, liberty and the pursuit of happiness.

The fact is, I'm not better than you, and you're not better than me.

We're equals.

Equals that become better individuals, better unions, when we acknowledge the gifting that has been bestowed upon the other.

But we don't stop there.

We also go out of our way to embrace and comfort others when the weight of the world weighs them down.

I am your Compassionate Neighbor, the guy who lives with his family next door.

Love me.

Work with me.

Pray with me.

March with me.

The Bane of Their Disdain

Woke up this morning
With you lying next to me
That sparkle in your eye
Testimony
Getting here wasn't boring
But it has been a chore
Having to proclaim to the naysayers
Disdain, no more

They have a problem
With us being together
Say our skin tones don't match
So our feelings don't matter
But I hold your hand tighter
When we're walking down the street
Enjoying your companionship
Oh, what a treat.

This caste system they created
That person better than the other
But all we ever wanted
Was to be the best of friends, lovers

All they had to do
Was leave us alone
To pursue life, liberty, happiness
Instead of picking at the bone

The bane of their disdain
Is the colors of our skin
But by harboring these sentiments
They succumb to unrighteousness, sin
Win hearts and minds
Save one's soul
Pray with me now
As we count the toll

Our union is a reminder
We're a community of equals
Placed on this planet
To pen our own prequels
For the stories that we tell ourselves
Isn't all that is written
Eternity beckons to us
Higher Power, smitten

They say the universe is expanding
Making room for the living, the dead
Death is not something
We're supposed to dread
With you by my side
My black skin pressed against your white
Walk confidently into eternity
Knowing our love for each other is right

Retreat of the Conquering Oppressor

You came.

You saw.

You conquered.

You oppressed.

But now you're reeling, from the impactful but nonviolent haymakers thrown in the 50s and 60s by Rosa Parks, Dr. Martin Luther King, Jr., Mamie Till-Bradley, John F. Kennedy,, Nina Simone, Malcolm X, Ruby Bridges, Lyndon B. Johnson and others.

You, Conquering Oppressor, are trying to hide your depraved state of mind...

....body...

...and soul...

...by telling anyone who will listen that your actions were, and continue to be, permissible because of our skin color, our allegedly being members of a subordinate and inferior caste.

But all you're doing now is hiding your crimes, the atrocities you committed, and continue to commit, against other human beings.

You know full well these crimes were, and are being, committed to advance your priorities, enrich yourself and individuals that look like you, the ones who wear their whiteness like a badge of honor.

We see you.

Or better said, we see right through you, a soul devoid of compassion, an unwillingness to embrace us, your more compassionate neighbors.

Do you ask yourself why we, your compassionate neighbors, remain compassionate, neighborly?

Why we default to nonviolence when it is within our right to violently lash out at you?

I'll tell you why.

We love you.

As siblings bound together by the blood of the risen Messiah, Jesus Christ.

And because our Lord and Savior is both merciful and transformative, we believe you have the capacity to change for the better.

Better means you, Conquering Oppressor, will come to recognize that your unrighteous acts are driven by hatred, buoyed by a superiority complex.

Better means you, Conquering Oppressor, cannot go it alone, that creating a more perfect union is an all-hands-on-deck proposition.

Better means you, Conquering Oppressor, must develop the capacity to love again, to be faithful to our God, kind to your neighbors.

We see that you're repulsed by what we're saying.

We see that you want to retreat to the silo that prevents you from hearing the wise counsel of the compassionate and the neighborly.

But actions speak louder than words.

That's why we stand before you now, arms spread wide, waiting for you to step forward into our hearty embrace.

We see those tears, a testament to your newfound compassion wanting to see the light of day.

Take that first step, toward us, your compassionate neighbors.

Accept this kiss to your cheek as I accept the one you're applying to mine.

Redemption feels good, doesn't it?

Welcome to God's More Perfect Union.

Kamala, Speak!

Call Joe Brandon
And his right eye glows
Lies about the legitimacy of his victory
The lowest of blows
He may be 80 years young
Slow with his speech
But when he says, "Build Back Better"
I respond, "Preach, brother, preach!"

Kamala Harris is Joe's
Second in command
A team marked by decency, integrity
In high demand
The other side stands with a man
Who aimed to enrich himself
Falsely claimed an election was stolen
Placing democracy on the shelf

In a few short months
We will go to the polls
But before we cast our ballots
We must first save some souls
They have the nerve to think
Their man has a chance

But the verdict is in
He's not deserving of their glance

Kamala, speak
We need to hear your voice
Too many Americans are prepared
To make the wrong choice
The electorate is waiting on the Democrats
To prosecute the case
Special counselors function independently
They're not part of the base

You interrogated witnesses
For Agent Orange was impeached twice
You turned to the cameras
Explaining why his actions weren't nice
You added that elected leaders represent
Both Republican and Democrat
He wants to create a narrative
Portray Joe as a feckless bureaucrat

The longer you remain silent
More lies he will spread
Narratives without merit
Intended to ferment dread
You are our avenging angel
To one of the highest offices elected
Express your judicial prowess now
Prevent this fool from being selected

He made his bed
Evaded taxes, found liable of rape
Kamala, my dear
It's time to put on your cape

Classified documents hoarded
Election tampering, hush money
Call him out for what he is
A con man, a phony

Now That You Know

Now that you know, what are you going to do? Knowing our being different is not a curse but a blessing. Mistakes have been made, lives have been lost, just so we could get here, to the Age of Enlightenment. But now that we're here, I'll ask again, what are you going to do? Will you acknowledge the common ground on which we stand? Will you turn the other cheek? Will you lash out in anger, verbally at first, then physically? I see the fire burning brightly in your eyes. I possess it too. But that smile on your face is a contagion, an invitation to continue our growth, together.

Mic Drop

First, thank you for this opportunity
To share one thought
About the banning of books
Diverse perspectives sought
This effort has nothing to do
With white children weeping
And everything to do
With black people seeping

Through glass ceiling placed there
To deny them access to liberty
Past the red lines on maps
To deny them passports to neighborly
But that's what we need
To set things right
And the books that we read
Allow us to gain invaluable insight

Black children weep
Each time they step inside our schools
So, don't sit there stoically
Thinking we're fools
Banning books written
By Ibram and Nikole

Impairing critical thinking skills
Hardening of the heart, soul

It's not like we haven't read
This script before
When Hitler did it
We said never again, no more
But here we are
In 2024
Asking if books about race
Should even be sold in the neighborhood store

That glare is intimidating
That expression smug
You must think you're winning
High on some drug
But we all end up losing
When you persist in playing games
Only a fool goes through life thinking
Our history is the same

Race is something
Your white ancestors created
To keep black people subservient
So outdated
My ancestors were brought to this country
Against their will
Now, you don't want us to talk about it
This stance you're taking can't be real

Moms for Liberty
Conservative activists all
Watch out now
You're about to stumble, fall

WOKE ideology
Is nothing new
It's what perfects our union
Keeps our states blue

I Am

I am a man
I am a hue-man
I am human

I am a husband
I am a father
I am a son

I am part of a collective
I am part of a nation
I am part of a world

I am a concerned citizen
I am a problem solver
I am a social entrepreneur

I am loved
I am collaborative
I am much more

More than who and what I am

Social Work

Help people help themselves
Easier said, harder done
Some people are stubborn
Living life like they've won
You see the people I encounter
Have problems galore
Addictions, traumatic experiences,
Homelessness and more

Our leaders in Washington
Say they want to lend a hand
But when they're elected to office
They put their heads in the sand
The voices that they listen to
Are the lobbyists, the pundits
Constituents' lives become chaotic
Finger pointing, whodunnit

Those who have made it
Should help the hungry, the lost
Stop spending so much time
Calculating the cost
Social Work requires a people
To show that they care

Simple acts of kindness
Don't just sit, stare

America can be great
But not filled with hatred, derision
A few bad apples
Telling lies, sowing division
We must call these bad apples out
In the corner, they must stand
They must change their wayward ways
Before being reunited with the band

Purpose must be found
In all that we do
Turn frowns into smiles
Is my commission to you
That smile means they're happy
That their trajectory is right
You actually being selfless
Not just suggesting you might

Let's commit to each other
To leave no one behind
An agape love that is enduring
Is the thing we must find
Old mentoring young
Maintaining long-held traditions
Young building upon old lessons
Becoming philanthropic champions

Peacemakers Wanted, Apply Within

Right now, there are two wars being waged - one in Ukraine, the other along the Gaza Strip.

The war in Ukraine was unprovoked, prompted by a dictator who feels the Ukrainian territory belongs to Autocratic Russia not the Democratic West.

The war along the Gaza Strip was provoked, as innocent Israeli residents were murdered, abducted as hostages. By Hamas, a recognized terrorist group.

Everyone agrees that Israel has a right to defend itself.

But why do we fight, wage senseless wars?

Why can't we all just get along, default to peace instead of perpetual chaos?

I see the televised images of displaced citizens and weary soldiers.

The displaced citizens want to return to their homes, enjoy the company of their family, relatives and friends. Their homes have been reduced to rubble and ash, but they don't care. They long for a return to where their hearts are.

The weary Ukrainian and Russian soldiers know this is a case of brother fighting brother. The only person who cares if the other is Autocratic or Democratic is the Russian autocrat calling the shots from the comforts of Moscow. But the Russian autocrat and his acolytes blindly press onward, naively believing they can re-chain former compatriots who have been savoring the flavors of democracy and freedom.

The Palestinian people don't pledge their allegiance to Hamas. They long for undisputed sovereignty, boundaries that Israel should not be permitted to infringe upon.

Therefore, we must bring an end to senseless wars by taking stock of our collective history, vowing to heed hard lessons learned from mistakes made during our chaotic past.

The world is split into continents and nations.

Differences – person, cultural and ideological – will always be with us.

But governments exist to establish and maintain rules of human engagement while fully acknowledging personal, cultural and ideological differences.

The solution.

Promote the peacemakers to consequential leadership positions...

...and demote the warmongers who rustle at the idea of a global utopia.

Lean Forward, Engage

Loud cheers rang out
When you took the stage
Our first black president
Urging us to lean forward, engage
Better days ahead
Same page, common talk
Chanting, "Yes we can!"
Compassionate Americans, walk

First hundred days
You focused on constituent health
But Conservative Republicans wanted you
To generate more wealth
For people who didn't see a need
To help the hungry and the sick
Their first priority
Generate an economic uptick

After they took control
Of the Senate and the House
They thought you would shrink away
Become a timid, little mouse
You had prevented a recession
Subdued international terrorists too

And even after all that
They thought you were through

You weren't through, though
You wanted to do more
But the people you were working with
Became rotten to the core
Lie, cheat, steal
That's what they blatantly did to win
Obstructing legislative remedies
Making all our heads spin

They then promoted a man
Who grabs women down low
After this became known
Hillary couldn't deliver the knockout blow
The promoted man had a plan
For making people mad
Called your presidency illegitimate
Which made his supporters glad

It always goes back
To what made America great
A black man elected president?
Hard for them to relate
In a country that was founded
For people with white skin
Their White Knight was promoted
Despite the popular vote he didn't win

Looking back on those days
You going high when they went low
Turning you into a racial avatar
White resentment, the defining blow

But now that we see
The writing on the wall
It's time for Woke Americans
To answer the call

They're trying to erase your legacy
Make it seem as if you did nothing
But when you became president
The Compassionate had done something
Never giving up
On wanting to become more
This racial animus citizens feel
Being extracted from America's core

Uncommitted

A campaign to send a message, one that pushes the duly elected U.S. president to demand a ceasefire along the Gaza Strip. What you fail to realize is he's not the one calling the shots, the Israeli president is. And he's on a mission to reshape the region to benefit Israel alone, not create a two-state solution. Everyone agrees that Israel has a right to defend itself, but Palestinian citizens aren't enemies, they're neighbors. Stop targeting their homes, schools and hospitals. Target hearts, minds, souls on both sides of the ideological divide. Righteous words and deeds signify that one has compassion for all in his heart.

Two Words

You sit there quietly, staring at a blank page. But you're spent, ambivalent, having a difficult time typing the words that need to be typed. You accepted this assignment, knowing that it was going to be a grind - testing your patience, adding layers of frustration and disappointment. You know you can only help people who want to be helped. Some of them were open, others were not. You know now that it wasn't them, it was the people leading you, the people who expected you to walk on water the day after giving your all. Two words. I quit.

Charge to the Compassionate Coalition

Dr. King has been admonishing us to come together as one since the 1950s.

Come together as brothers or die together as fools, he once said.

But here we are, seventy-four years after he made his first rousing speech, trying to determine if we will allow complacency to replace compassion.

For me, the answer is obvious. I choose to be compassionate, not complacent. But so many others have chosen the latter, thinking complacency will heal the racial divide, prevent the nation's marginalized groups from finally experiencing the rights of full US citizenship.

I blame established religions for this frantic march toward complacency. They have hitched their carts to an ideology that appeals more to their selfishness, less to their selflessness.

The Christian Church is the worst. They have captive audiences every Sunday morning, and once during the week, on Wednesdays, and they still choose not to denounce a presidential candidate who once joked about people looking the other way after he touches women's vaginas without their consent.

What's worse, some denominations within the Christian Church believe he was sent by God to do God's bidding. But truth be told, the things he has said, the actions he has taken, have nothing to do with what God wants and are more about everything selfishly unrighteous that the presidential candidate wants.

But this problem is bigger than one man. It has a lot to do with how we interact with each other.

We don't. At least not well.

We're more attached to our smart phones and tablets than ever before, and while we acquire a tremendous amount of information from them, we pick and choose those coals of information that coincide more perfectly with our individual world views.

We must ask ourselves, why are we choosing the blackened coals over the golden nuggets?

Have our minds become so depraved that we can no longer sense the urgency of now?

In 2008, US voters elected the first, Black male President.

In 2020, US voters elected the first, Black female Vice President.

Both candidates represented the Democratic Party, which has a history of not being too kind to persons of color.

Let's reflect on these moments, how we felt seeing two descendants of an enslaved, oppressed and marginalized group rising to become leaders of the free world, as Democrats.

At this nation's core is a desire to become a More Perfect Union. In the words of Black motorist Rodney King, we should all just do our part to "get along" with others.

But for that to happen, for us to get along, we must drown out, not silence, the voices spewing messages of hatred and division rather than love and unity.

We must hold the ordained Purveyors of Love and Truth to account, letting them know an unenlightened segment of their leadership and congregations are sleeping at the wheel, allowing the Purveyors of Hatred and Lies to ferment a More Imperfect Union.

We should be wary of leaders who condone the banning of books that enhance the critical thinking skills of children and adults.

We should be wary of leaders who prevent refugees from legitimately pursuing asylum, pathways to US citizenship.

Lastly, we should be wary of leaders who enact laws to regulate women's bodies, denying women opportunities to decide what they want to do with their bodies in consultation with trained, medical professionals.

Embrace your wokeness, Compassionate Coalition. It's not a bad thing.

And being woke, or enlightened, is nothing new. It has always been there, this feeling of being fully aware of what is morally right and good for everyone, not just a select few.

In November 2024, vote for candidates who privately and publicly stand on the side of moral enlightenment, unconditional love, equal justice and inconvenient truth.

Do this, and our transformation into a More Perfect Union will resume, as our words and deeds will show that more of us are guided by the love and compassion in our hearts.

The Magnificence of Your Singleness

Fond memories I have
Of our life together,
The magnificence of your singleness.

You worked tirelessly
To keep a roof overhead,
Clothes on our backs.

And now I marvel
At what your singleness
Has wrought.

Three young'uns, college graduates all.
Discovered love with three beautiful souls,
Bore children of their own.

Yes, we had help from our soulmates,
But you are in us,
In our ambitious and hardworking children.

As a child, I prayed that you
Would find someone

To love you back.

The same way you love
On others.
Selah!

But that person never arrived,
To receive the gift of
A blended life with you.

Know this:
We have always been here,
And you have never been alone.

Balance

There's this quote that says, "We find balance by losing it."

At first glance, I had no idea what it meant. But now, I find myself digging, deeper, in an attempt to understand what losing it means.

Balance is a word that can be superimposed with the word control. But what are we, as humans, trying to control.

As a poet and a writer, I reign supreme over my words, endeavoring to tell stories that represent my interpretations of how people should interact in places and with things. In short, I put characters in situations filled with complications, and in the end, my characters overcome the obstacles I put in their way.

But this is not reality, it is fiction, a wish really, for how I want the world to be, how I want the people in my world to be. In reality, though, people are going to be who and what they want to be, maintaining full control of their own destinies.

What many fail to realize is these destinies are tied together, what impacts one may, at times, impact the other. Therefore, as you wrap your arms around my waist from behind, you have to feel me, I you, so the bicycle that bears the brunt of our weight doesn't tumble over, fall.

We must find that common space, an assurance really, that the one has the other. The destination has already been set, peace and tranquility await, and the only forces that will give us the inertia to move forward together are patience and kindness.

We must not hold a grudge against the other. We must learn to love again, and always. This love must be unconditional and enduring, because in the end, all we have is each other.

Able

When I complained
About my injury,
Not being able to compete,
I watched you
Limp over to me,
A smirk on your face.

You placed your dark hand
On my shoulder near the finish line
As you peered into
My tear-drenched eyes.

I had pulled up lame,
Hamstring tear.

But you told me
I was gifted,
That I would heal,
Run again.

Tinged with these
Words of encouragement
Was a gentle reminder,
That some people feel blessed,

Just to stand upright,
To walk with
The slightest of limp.

I did run again,
Compete.

But where you
Called me gifted,
I remember you
Giving me a gift,
An appreciation really
Of knowing forward movement
Isn't sustained in the wake of
Of sadness and loss.

It is maintained,
Strengthened, by
Right thinking,
Right thoughts.

Critical Race Theory

Professor Kimberlé Crenshaw
Say you right
Pointing out the obvious,
Their reliance on sight
Concept of race,
Created by them
The collective power of others,
They endeavor to stem

Her ideas are grounded
In the critiques of Derrick Bell
Who thought Brown v. Board
Was symbolic, subverting racism's swell
Use litigation to
Overcome historical discrimination
Let the conquering oppressors know
They're not exempt from incrimination

Lie, cheat, steal
To occupy the top spot
Now the roosters are crowing,
Their racist antics they blot
Crenshaw's seminal text explains
The legal ramifications of race,

Reconcile abuses together,
Buffeted by transformative grace

Critical Race Theory,
The subject of debates
Our civil rights struggle on trial,
Revisitation of their worst traits
State of being,
State of mind
Not wanting the resentful among them
To find the will to be compassionate, kind

Much pride they once had
Being the party of Lincoln
Granted freedom to Blacks,
Now they are sinking
They equate CRT
with DEI,
Reversing decades of hard work,
Meant to make us rectify

Resentful Whites convinced
The problem is Woke
But Woke ideology isn't the problem,
Racial animus they stoke
They're conditioning your minds
To ignore research, facts
Embrace the privileges of whiteness,
Not their ancestors' criminal acts

Diversity, equity, inclusion,
The programs that we need
Republican governors cutting them,
Unearthing the seed

Seed that prompts discussion
About unfathomable sin
Persons of color the victims,
Always wanting us all to win

Woke White Americans
Marching in lockstep with us
Blacks, Natives, Hispanics, Asians,
United, not making a fuss.
Immigrants all, we strive daily
To carve out a space
Where we embrace our siblings,
Not predicated on ethnicity, race

Our humanity is what should
Bind us together as one
Love and compassion for each other,
Sipping iced tea under the sun
The stories that we tell ourselves
Must be true
Extending kindness to others,
Not allowing resentments to brew

Two Sides, Two Coins

When speaking about politics, they say political party candidates represent two sides of the same coin.

I beg to differ.

They're not.

If anything, they're two sides of different coins.

One coin has two sides that value conquest and oppression.

The other coin has two sides that value compassion and being neighborly.

I prefer the latter.

And you should too.

"Why?" you ask.

Thank you for the question.

But you may not like my answer, the resounding truth engrained in my words.

No matter your color...

...no matter your race...

...no matter your ethnicity,

...we all are susceptible to the entanglements of the Conquering Oppressor Mindset.

The Conquering Oppressor fully embraces the belief that says he is better than everyone else, supreme, and that his betterment and supremacy are ordained by God.

The Conquering Oppressor fully embraces the unmerited privileges inherited from his ancestors' conquest and oppression of people considered less than, inferior to, him.

The Conquering Oppressor fully embraces his obligation to protect these unmerited privileges, to fend off any and all attacks on his self-ordained supremacy.

The Compassionate Neighbor is different.

The Compassionate Neighbor fully embraces the belief that she is equal to, not better than, everyone else, and that her equality with others requires her to see God's goodness in all, not just a select few.

The Compassionate Neighbor fully embraces a tainted historical record, her obligation to enact policies and practices that correct the destructive legacy of her predecessors.

The Compassionate Neighbor fully embraces the fact that the only privileges that matter are the ones emanating from her blood, sweat and tears, her toil.

She extends her hand backwards and downward to lift up her neighbors so she can draw them close for a long, hearty embrace and deliver reassuring whispers that all will be well.

What damage the Conquering Oppressor has wrought.

Enslavement and oppression of native Africans and their descendants.

Attempted erasure of African and African American achievement and excellence.

Banned books written to prompt much-needed discussion about the healing of old relational wounds.

We deserve leaders who show through their righteous words and deeds that they are more Compassionate Neighbor than Conquering Oppressor.

But here's the test.

Are they doing unto others as they would have others do unto them?

Are they collaborating with others to find common ground?

More than anything, are their actions guided by love and compassion for their neighbors?

Anyone failing this test should not be elevated to positions of leadership or responsibility.

They should be demoted to the fires of irrelevancy and obscurity.

Wakanda Dreaming

T'challa, the Black Panther,
Was created in 1966
By Kirby and Lee.
But 48 years later,
We draw inspiration from this character,
Brighter destiny.
Do I wish the Black Panther
Was created
By two Black guys?
Yes, I do.
Afro-futurism by us
So we can reach new highs.

When I close my eyes,
Wakanda dreams
Consume the recesses of my mind.
Tech-savvy Black people,
Occupying unseen African territory,
Yet refusing to be blind.
They never experienced
The unwelcome overtures
Of the colonizing Brit
They relied exclusively on
Their devotion to each other,

Their tireless grit.

Black Wall Street.
Black Americans
At their best.
Reconstruction era,
1863 to 1877.
No time to rest.
Wakanda in real time,
Tulsa's Greenwood District
Wasn't a dream.
But ever since
The 1921 Tulsa Massacre,
Black people have been losing some steam.

School suspensions,
Incarcerations,
To paint all Black people as bad.
Justification for their ancestors'
Cruelty against us,
Attempts to make us mad.
More of us must excel
In the classroom,
On the job too.
We define who we are,
The amount of respect, power,
That we subdue.

My charge to Black America
Is go high when they
Go low
The successes
That we achieve,
What a mighty blow.

Life is not a competition,
A sprint to
The finish line.
Life is about selfless giving,
Assurances
That everything will be fine.

Wakanda can be real
If we replace nods
With a coherent plan.
Black people working together
To get from under the foot
Of the man.
If we dream it,
We can be it.
Build upon ancestral gains.
Draw strength and inspiration
From Wakanda dreams,
The Civil Rights legacy that remains.

TRUE BUILD | A
Black Wall Street Story

Principal Newman wasn't happy. His pale face was ashen behind a set of rosy cheeks, and a clear sheen of sweat covered his balding head and brow. Winston sat directly in front of him, on the other side of the mahogany desk, his hands clasped together in his lap. Julia Ball, the district's legal counsel, sat in a chair to the right of Winston, listening, leaning ever so close to him as not to miss his retorts to Principal Newman's line of questioning.

"Why would you say such a thing?" Principal Newman asked from a seated position behind his desk. "To a classroom full of impressionable ninth graders? Are you even paying attention to the news reports, what their parents are saying about us?"

Winston leaned back in his chair, undeniably confounded by the forcefulness of Principal Newman's assertion. Winston was fully aware of the heated exchanges that had been occurring between school board members and the parents of Loudoun County students. But he had also surmised that conservative Republican operatives had embedded themselves into these audiences and were largely responsible for turning the monthly school board meetings into circuses, bastions for the dissemination of half-truths, lies and disinformation.

Winston only had one year of teaching under his belt. And that first year went by without a hitch. But the more the Republican presidential incumbent used his public rallies to rail against teachers like him, the more he realized he had to stop being so loose with his words. In 2020, the incumbent Republican president was running for a second term, against the Democratic Party's nominee, and the incumbent Republican president had shown that he would remain undeterred in openly berating public school administrators and their faculty for teaching K-12 students what he and so many other conservative Republicans considered wrong lessons about race.

"I am," Winston replied. "But I stand by my statement. Black Americans are the true builders of opportunity and sustainable success."

"But that's not true, Winston, and you know it. Don't get me wrong. You Blacks have had a lot to overcome. But for a highly intelligent Black man like you to tell a room full of White kids that. That's a bit much, don't you think?"

Winston immediately countered, at least in his mind, with, "That's rich." Better to think it than say it out loud.

"Winston," Julia interjected, using her right hand to brush a few strands of her blonde hair off her face. "We're not here to be overly critical of you, as a teacher. Your students love you. Your colleagues love you. But our parents are questioning what their children are being taught in your class about race. And while the claim that Critical Race Theory is being taught in K through twelve classrooms is ridiculous, the fact remains that there are elected officials – all conservative Republicans, mind you – on the local, state, and national levels who are legitimizing it in hopes of peeling away a few votes from the Dems during the upcoming elections."

"And I get that," Winston said, a hint of exasperation in his voice. "But the only critical thing I'm trying to teach my students is to think critically about American history. They don't have to take what I say at face value. But my hope is they fully process what I am trying to communicate to them. I want them to leave class wanting to do their own research. I want them to have an appreciation for the complete historical record, paying attention to all its blemishes."

"And we respect that," said Principal Newman. He stood and walked around to the front of his desk. He was now a mere six feet from

Winston, three from Julia. He sat on the edge of his desk to look down at Winston.

"It's a Friday, Winston," Principal Newman exclaimed, his right eye twitching once, maybe twice, as he spoke. "Having to talk with you about this bullshit is the last thing I wanted to do today." He stood, stepped to his right. "But go home. Use the weekend to think about how uncomfortable your words made the White students in your class feel."

Winston raked his hand across the full length of his face before leaning back once more, thumbing the sides of the wooden chair. He had not become an educator – more specifically a history teacher – to make his White students feel comfortable. He knew, like so many other educators, that if one is to teach true American history, the hearers of what is being taught must have the capacity to deal with its undertones.

However, the fact that his boss got up out of his chair to remove the barrier between them, let him know that he sincerely wanted Winston to remain on staff. But that would require that he toe any line Principal Newman set for him moving forward. Therefore, Winston stood, extended his hand. Principal Newman met and clamped down on it in midair, holding it steady in the space between them.

"I will," Winston said as he shook his hand free. Then, backing away toward the exit door, he added, "See you on Monday?"

Principal Newman replied, "Yes. See you on Monday."

~

That night, sometime between eight and nine, Winston found himself stretched out on his living room sofa, feet propped up on the coffee table, as he flipped through the pages of a book titled The 1619 Project. The last slice of a pizza grew cold in a box on the dining room table, basking under the glow of chandelier lights. The seven other slices had been good enough for Winston, at least for now. The sound of an explosion made him look over at the wall-mounted television across the room, increasing the anxiety he was feeling about the real possibility of losing his teaching job.

He already had a sense of who ratted him out. It could have only been one of two suspects – Johnny Richards or Pamela Towns. Johnny didn't say much in class, but when he did, his classmates seemed to hang on his every word. Pamela, on the other hand, was very outspoken in class, and Winston could tell she was a "my way or no way" kind of girl. But he also knew Johnny's parents' politics ran counter to his own. Therefore, if he were a betting man, he would put all his chips on Suspect Number One.

And for good reason. When Johnny, a new student, stepped into his classroom during the middle of the 2021-22 school year, after the school's Winter break, he proudly announced to everyone within ear-shot that in 2016 his parents had voted for the Republican presidential incumbent, who was then the Republican presidential nominee. It didn't matter that the man bragged about how the women he knew loved it when he grabbed them by their pussies. And it didn't matter that he told reporters that there are good people on "both sides" after one of those "good" White supremacists ended a White BLM protestor's life by running her over with his car. All that seemed to matter to Johnny's parents, and Johnny as their child, was the belief that the Republican presidential incumbent could do no wrong because all he wanted to do was "make America great again."

Winston chuckled to himself at the intended cockiness of this statement. He knew no one president, or political party for that matter, could truly make America great again. All he, or she, or even they, could hope to do is do what their predecessors had committed themselves to doing, which was to create a more perfect union. The last time Winston checked, creating a more perfect union was the corporate vision laid out in both the U.S. Constitution and Declaration of Independence. Now, he wondered how this truth had become lost on the Republican presidential incumbent, Congressional Republican legislators, and the six Republican Supreme Court justices.

Winston had a more difficult time reading Pamela. She considered the Second Amendment, the right to bear arms, sacred, and she was an outspoken critic of abortion rights. She believed that persons kill people, not the arms they bear. Consequently, she felt all the United States government, in collaboration with the Christian church, had to do was win the hearts and minds of gun purchasers, keep guns out of the hands of citizens with psychological problems. Pamela also believed that life begins at conception. But when it came to same-sex marriage, her views seemingly became more liberal and less conservative.

When her gay and lesbian classmates reminisced aloud during classroom discussions about the 2016 Pulse Nightclub shooting in Orlando, Florida, in which 49 people were killed, another 53 injured, Pamela defended them. These classmates talked about how they are now scared to openly display any type of affection toward their same-sex partners. Pamela now believed that people should be able to love whomever they wanted to love, whether male, female, or nonbinary. But Winston had heard from Issac, another Black man who just happened to be the school's Physical Plant director, that Pamela had extra motivation for her defense. He divulged that a female member of his janitorial staff caught Pamela and another White girl, Leslie Cooper, French kissing and feeling each other up under the gymnasium bleachers about a month before Winston was called into Principal Newman's office.

Winston peered over at the wall clock on the far side of the room. Nine fifteen. He opened The 1619 Project book once more, with every intention of reading Nikole Hannah-Jones' piece on Justice. However, as his eyes soaked in the words on the chapter's first page, he could feel them getting heavier. Not long after that, they were completely shut, his nostrils flaring from the forcefulness of his snores. When his eyes opened, he was...

~

...sitting in a barber's chair, his upper body covered by a barber's cape from the neck down.

"They know Dick didn't do nothing wrong," said Sammy, the establishment's proprietor. Sammy, his round belly fighting to stay under his waist-length barber's smock, took great care in using a pair of scissors to put the finishing touches on Winston's cut. There were about five other Black men sitting in chairs in front of and around Winston. Others sat patiently in the two rows of chairs positioned in front of the plate-glass window with Sammy's Barbershop painted on it on the outside. "But Hubert and his boys down at the courthouse now. Making sure those crackers don't take Dick out back to hang his ass."

A light-skinned brother getting his hair cut to Winston's right shifted in his chair, causing his barber Damon to take a momentary pause.

"I told him not to go down there," the light-skinned brother exclaimed. "At least not armed. Told him some of the White folks around here don't take too kindly to what we have going on over here, in Greenwood. I been hearing rumblings around town, how they scheming to take all this away from us."

Another man sitting in a chair on the front left row of the chairs interjected, asking, "How they going to do that O.W.?" He uncrossed his legs and spread them wide. "You and J.D. purchased Greenwood outright," he continued, gesturing with his hands for emphasis. "All of us working together is what turned it into a thriving community. So, I'm sorry. We built this, not them."

"We did, Clive," O.W. replied. "But some of us are getting caught up, drawing too much attention to what we built. That White girl down at the Drexel Building done come out and said Dick stumbled and accidentally stepped on her foot. But them White boys still lying about the whole thing, saying he attacked her. Makes you wonder what they plan on doing to the rest of us."

Just as O.W. mouthed these words, the plate glass window to his right imploded, causing shards of glass to rain down on the row of seated patrons. All eyes followed the trajectory of a large brick as it flew over their heads and bounced across the floor. Seconds later, they watched again as a Coke bottle with a flaming makeshift wick flew through the open space to splatter trails of kerosene and flame across the room.

Winston ripped the kerosene-soaked cape from around his neck and tossed it toward the billowing flames. It became ash before it could hit the floor. He then hastily followed Sammy, O.W. and the others to the back storeroom. Once there, they all exited through a door that led to the back alley. But once he was outside, Winston froze.

O.W. briefly stood with Winston before trotting away. Before getting too far, he peered back at Winston. He motioned to Winston. O.W. watched as Winston seemed to recognize the urgency of now. So, when Winston caught up to O.W., they wasted little time retreating down the shadowed alleyway.

Night had fallen on the Greenwood District, and all Greater Tulsa for that matter, but the full moon and the flames rifting from the burning buildings provided enough lighting for them to get around. But when O.W. and Winston reached one of the main streets, they found themselves walking past the dead bodies of Black, and a few White and Native American, Greenwood residents. A mix of splatters and pools of dark, red blood surrounded the bodies, many of them riddled with gunshot wounds. Overwhelmed by it all, Winston froze again, almost falling to his knees.

"Come on, young buck," O.W. pleaded, as he prepared to take a left onto an adjoining street "They still out there. Hunting."

But before Winston could get back to his feet, a tall White man dressed in denim overalls, carrying a shotgun, rounded the corner of a brick building. When he spotted Winston, he raised his shotgun, finger on the trigger, taking aim. Fortunately for Winston, O.W. got him first. A single shot to the back of the White man's head from O.W.'s revolver sent the White man reeling face first onto the dirt turf.

"Let's go," said O.W., slipping the revolver back into the shoulder holster hidden under the confines of his suit jacket. "They're waiting."

The further they walked away from Greenwood, the darker it became. A thin line of sunlight peeked over the horizon to the east. Moonlight allowed Winston to make out the trees, bushes and vines that stood between them and their destination. But those darn thorn bushes caused him to wince as they tore into the exposed skin around his hands and forearms. Winston kept telling himself that he was born for conditions like this. Frolicking around the woods as a child with his friends used to be an everyday occurrence during the summer months.

Of course, he knew the armed White mob was rumbling through Greenwood's dusty streets, frothing from their mouths at the mere thought of destroying everyone and everything that had a connection to Greenwood. It was then that Winston realized he was indeed a man out of place, out of time.

"You're O.W. Gurley, aren't you?" asked Winston when they stopped briefly to catch their breaths.

O.W. replied, "I am. And you are?"

"Winston. Winston James."

"Pleasure meeting you, Winston James."

Winston flopped to his bottom and allowed his back to rest against a large oak tree. "Seems like we been running for hours, sir. Where we going?"

O.W. joined Winston under the tree but opted to remain standing. He pulled a handkerchief from his inside pocket, using it to dab at his brow. "Somewhere safe, Winston. A gathering place."

Winston peered at O.W., admiring how O.W.'s pale face was shrouded in light and darkness. As a student of Black American history, Winston knew a little about the role gathering places played in helping his enslaved ancestors develop a sense of identity and purpose. And while these gathering places were used mostly to practice their version of Christianity beyond the oversight of White overseers, the frustrated and anxious Black men of that bygone era used them to plan, coordinate and execute a somewhat radical form of activism that would one day win them their freedom.

Moments later, Winston, once again, found himself falling in lock-step with O.W. for what Winston hoped was the final leg of their journey. However, the sound of barking dogs and the sight of lit torches caused them to take refuge behind a row of bushes. When the dogs' barks became growls mixed with the slopping sounds of flesh being ripped from bone, Winston knew one of this White crews had caught up to some Greenwood residents. And by the sound of things, the dogs wasted very little time making mincemeat of their captives, buoyed by the urgings of their White owners. Then, five thunderous claps from a shotgun rang out.

With the White crew and their dogs moving further down the road, Winston and O.W. emerged from their hiding place. They were headed in the same direction as the crime scene, so there was no avoiding the carnage wrought by the rabid dogs and their White owners. As they drew closer, O.W. turned slightly away from the piles of ripped flesh and exposed bone, looking instead toward the heavens, seeking comfort wherever any could be found. Winston could tell O.W. recognized the four lifeless bodies – A Black man and woman, their two elementary school-aged children. Tragically reduced to nothing more than empty vessels.

"Dem bastards," muttered O.W. Then, from a squatting position, inches from what appeared to be the Black father, he extended his right hand, and with his thumb and index finger, he forced the Black father's eyes shut. If only he could have done the same for the others. But how could he? Deep, bloody holes and indentions now occupied the spaces where the mother and children's faces had been.

Winston surmised that two members of the White crew had probably forced the Black father to his knees as they shot his wife and children in their faces with their shotguns. Images of them standing the Black father up and then riddling his battered but not broken body with bullets played in Winston's mind. All to show the Black father that they were the one's wielding absolute power absolutely, he thought.

O.W. rose from his stooping position to stand tall with his head tilted toward the full moon. Down but not beaten. Then, without saying a word, he took a single glance at Winston, seemingly to see if he was still engaged.

Winston found himself following O.W. as he crawled into what appeared to be a large hole on the side of a rolling hill. The hole was covered with foliage with a thick row of bushes to its left, so one had to know what he was looking for to find it. O.W. was definitely in the know. Winston entered behind O.W. Once inside, he stood upright, his eyes widening at the spectacle before him. They were now in a spacious cavern, the only lighting coming from fiery flames atop torches that had been secured high in the crevices of the cavern's stony walls.

Winston spotted O.W. greeting, tightly embracing and then releasing a dark-skinned brother to his right. Several feet to his left, the eyes of what appeared to be some of Greenwood's displaced residents looked back at him. The displaced sat three or four rows deep in multiple huddles throughout the cavern. Winston surmised that their numbers included more Black bodies than others. But as he surveyed their downcast faces, Winston was pleased to see Greenwood residents of Native American, Asian and Caucasian descent sitting among the displaced. This was the Greenwood that the history books didn't tell you about, Winston thought. A coalition as colorful as the rainbow, built by Black entrepreneurs to uplift the Black race while simultaneously being open to conducting business with anyone willing to sufficiently compensate hardworking Greenwood residents for their labor.

O.W. motioned to Winston as he and the dark-skinned brother solemnly walked toward a stony enclave situated in the right-hand corner of the cavern. Winston spotted Sammy and two other Black men that he had seen earlier at the barbershop sitting inside, around a blazing fire.

O.W. and Winston sat with the others around the fire. The dark-skinned brother did the same. "This here J.D. J.D. Stradford."

Winston nodded at J.D. as he settled in around the fire.

"He the one that helped me do all this," O.W. continued. J.D.'s gaze shifted from Winston to the logs burning in the fire. "Amazing what we were able to accomplish."

Winston sat patiently, waiting for J.D. to say something, anything, to him. But J.D. remained silent as the tears mounted in his eyelids to roll down the sides of his ebony cheeks.

"All we ever wanted to do was create a better life for ourselves," he said, "for our people. We didn't ask them for nothing; just wanted to be left alone. But they couldn't even allow us to have that. What we built with our own blood, our own sweat, our own tears." He locked eyes with O.W. "They done took it from us, O.W. What we going to do now?"

O.W.'s gaze retreated from J.D. to the faces of the other Black men seated around the fire. Then, while gazing into the fire, he replied, "We rebuild. And we keep rebuilding until they stop coming at us, after us. Sooner or later, they're going to get the message – that we're not going anywhere, that we're here to stay."

Winston closed his eyes to whisper a silent prayer. When they opened, he found himself...

~

...back in his living room, reclining on the sofa, The 1619 Project book lying open with the pages pressing into his chest.

Winston tilted The 1619 Project book up so he could pick up where he left off. His eyes immediately fell on the bolded words "Freed people" in the middle of the page. His interest piqued, he continued, reading, "...tried to compel the government to provide restitution for slavery, to provide at the very least a pension for those who, along with generations of their ancestors, had spent their entire lives toiling for no pay. They filed lawsuits. They organized to lobby politicians. And every effort failed."

Winston shifted his gaze from the page to the talking heads on the television across the room. Even though he was looking at them, he really was looking past them, at the faces of O.W. Gurley and J.D. Stradford staring back at him.

It saddened him that these two Black, self-made, American men had their dream of a self-sufficient Black American community scuttled by a White American populace that didn't have an appetite for Black people pursuing and achieving life, liberty and happiness, excellence even. His own analysis of what had transpired in Greenwood revealed that its Black American residents weren't filing lawsuits or lobbying politicians to get what they wanted, what they were entitled too. Hell, they could have cared less about receiving handouts from the Federal government. Again, they had legally purchased Midwestern land. Now, or least then, they wanted to be left alone so they could lead lives that were free of turmoil and strife.

~

Winston watched quietly as his students packed up their belongings and made a hasty exit through the door at the back of the classroom.

After most of them had cleared out, he used the remote to power off the smart board. But when he looked up, he spotted Johnny approaching.

"Hey, Mr. Winston," Johnny began, nervously tugging on the book-bag dangling from his shoulder. "Can we talk?"

"Sure," said Winston, dropping to the rolling ergonomic chair between his desk and the smart board.

"I owe you an apology, sir."

"An apology?" Winston said, feigning surprise. "For what?"

"For telling my parents about what you said in class last week."

"No worries, Johnny. No harm, no foul. I just hope your parents understand that I wasn't trying to be mean-spirited by saying what I said."

Johnny allowed his bookbag to slide off his back and drop to the floor. "That's the problem," he said, slipping into the desk chair directly in front of Winston's. "They act like they don't, but they do. They plan to make an issue out of it anyway. The school board has agreed to allow my mother to speak out against you at Wednesday's meeting." Winston swallowed hard. "I just want you to know, I do. I understand exactly what you were saying."

Johnny shifted his body and legs to lean sideways in the desk chair, his left elbow on his thigh, his right on the desktop. "I did my own research, sir. Like you always encourage us to do. Came up with my own conclusions. Black people have always been about the business of showing the rest of us what it truly means to be, well, American. Because of the way people that look like me used to treat Black people, America has never been great; it has always been a country in search of greatness. These MAGA people – my parents included – are trying to confuse the issue by referring to history that focuses on Black enslavement, oppression, and disenfranchisement as Critical Race Theory. They want to make White people think we have done enough to right our ancestors' wrongs. But we haven't. If anything, we have only been making things worse for everyone by ignoring the wrong things that we have done and keep doing to Black people." Johnny sat upright. "I just think too many of us are tone deaf, sir."

Winston allowed his backside to come into alignment with the contours of his ergonomic chair, his elbows on the right and left armrests, his hands coming together to form a bridge, inches from his face.

Johnny glanced up at Winston and then quickly looked away.

Winston stood, walked to the front of his desk. Once there, he offered his right hand to Johnny. When Johnny reached up and accepted it with his own, Winston pulled him up from the chair. The two stood there, for two or three ticks, eyeing each other in silence.

"You see," Winston began, "this here is what I'm talking about. Connection. You now see what I see, what I and my people experience or have experienced. And that, young buck, is the first step to building community, together."

Johnny nodded, smirking, as Winston patted him on the back.

Johnny felt fortunate to be in this number.

MEET THE POET

J. A. Faulkerson is a Creative Writer who develops projects that entertain, educate and enlighten. Through his writing, he hopes to inspire others to love more, hate less.

J. A. is available to speak about his insights and experiences as a Creative Writer, Child and Family Advocate, Social Entrepreneur, and Nonprofit Administrator.